SCAT

100 Verbal Analogies

for

Grades 2-5

Copyright ©2018 A Lee
All Rights Reserved
ISBN-13: 978-1987534252

ISBN-10: 1987534255
No part of this book may be reproduced
without written permission from the author.

for friends and family

TABLE OF CONTENTS

A Brief Introduction 5
Test 1 7
Test 2 17
Answers.. 25

A Brief Introduction

This book contains 100 carefully curated verbal analogies based on the sample questions and information from students who have successfully prepared and aced the test.

The book is divided into two tests, each with 50 analogies. The questions increase in difficulty as you approach the end of the test. Because you do not need to get everything right to pass the cutoff, do not get too discouraged.

Read the analogy carefully and go through each answer choice slowly. The SCAT questions are very tricky–these questions have been designed to be near identical to the ones you will find in the test. Enthusiastic and advanced 2nd and 3rd graders will find this book useful with proper guidance. 4th and 5th graders will find this to be challenging but within their reach.

Good luck!

Test 1

Directions

Each question begins with two words. These two words go together in a certain way. Under them, there are four other pairs of words lettered A, B, C, and D.

Find the lettered pair of words that go together in the same way as the first pair of words.

1 chalk : board ::
   A pencil : eraser
   B dog : tail
   C grass : green
   D pen : paper

2 simple : complex ::
   A great : hopeful
   B funny : hilarious
   C warm : cool
   D pretty : gorgeous

3 giant : dwarf ::
   A open : inside
   B vacation : busy
   C true : false
   D easy : perfect

4 snow : blizzard ::
   A winter : cold
   B ice : hard
   C rain : hurricane
   D nature : outside

5 kick : foot ::
   A shoot : soccer
   B toe : nail
   C chew : teeth
   D twist : turn

6 apple : fruit ::
   A tree : plant
   B flower : garden
   C cat : lion
   D beetle : horn

7   fork : spoon ::
    A   egg : shell
    B   piano : harp
    C   pig : bacon
    D   tiger : lion

8   socks : foot ::
    A   gloves : hand
    B   pants : belt
    C   hat : face
    D   shoelace : shoe

9   leaf : branch ::
    A   cap : head
    B   nose : smell
    C   finger : hand
    D   tail : leg

10 ship : captain ::
    A   car : passenger
    B   nanny : baby
    C   chef : kitchen
    D   airplane : pilot

11 tired : rest ::
    A   rested : lie
    B   sad : cry
    C   hungry : buy
    D   bored : watch

12 tongue : taste ::
    A   toe : stand
    B   ear : hear
    C   eye : blink
    D   hair : cover

13 drive : street ::
    A   fly : bird
    B   eat : snack
    C   run : school
    D   walk : path

14 violin : instrument ::
    A   animal : life
    B   museum : art
    C   bat : equipment
    D   pencil : paper

15 spider : web ::
   A office : chairs
   B school : student
   C field : snake
   D bird : nest

16 broom : sweep ::
   A mop : water
   B saw : sharp
   C hammer : nail
   D ruler : measure

17 bright : dazzling ::
   A good : excellent
   B loud : confusing
   C sunny : warm
   D noisy : silent

18 scared : terrified ::
   A confused : lost
   B mixed : sloppy
   C glad : thrilled
   D proud : brave

19 remember : past ::
   A plan : trip
   B forget : mistakes
   C write : thoughts
   D imagine : future

20 run : track ::
   A dive : beach
   B play : weekend
   C swim : pool
   D walk : sidewalk

21 doctor : treats ::
   A plumber : builds
   B actor : practices
   C teacher : instructs
   D police : drives

22 chair : furniture ::
   A song : music
   B carrot : vegetable
   C markers : tape
   D cord : telephone

23 weak : strength ::
    A smart : wisdom
    B private : secrets
    C strong : power
    D poor : wealth

24 computer : electricity ::
    A phone : charge
    B vitamin : nutrients
    C car : gas
    D kitchen : knives

25 dawn : dusk ::
    A scream : shriek
    B drink : eat
    C copy : trace
    D start : finish

26 wolf : pack ::
    A fish : tank
    B chicken : hen
    C cow : herd
    D team : players

27 messy : unorganized ::
    A tired : busy
    B distracted : focused
    C smart : lazy
    D courageous : brave

28 whisper : yell ::
    A smirk : frown
    B glance : stare
    C annoy : bother
    D carry : gather

29 president : country ::
    A chief : tribe
    B prince : kingdom
    C team : captain
    D emperor : city

30 flap : wing ::
    A speak : sound
    B stub : toe
    C wave : hand
    D whisper : word

31 poison : deadly ::
    A solid : liquid
    B medicine : locked
    C sugar : sweet
    D milk : carton

35 carpenter : woodwork ::
    A cook : heat
    B potter : shape
    C weaver : cloth
    D guitarist : strings

32 midnight : noon ::
    A dark : sunshine
    B angry : fearful
    C hungry : dinner
    D south : north

36 space : crowded ::
    A silence : noisy
    B sadness : funeral
    C smell : dirty
    D joy : happiness

33 word : letter ::
    A paragraph : sentence
    B chapter : book
    C comma : period
    D stanza : poem

37 story : building ::
    A layer : cake
    B balloon : circus
    C candle : birthday
    D root : plant

34 claw : cat ::
    A tail : mouse
    B whisker : beaver
    C hoof : horse
    D bell : cow

38 newspaper : inform ::
    A book : excite
    B park : entertain
    C show : distract
    D manual : instruct

39 test : score ::
  A homework : comment
  B teacher : lesson
  C essay : assignment
  D class : grade

43 terrified : scared ::
  A bored : excited
  B mad : bothered
  C depressed : sad
  D tired : rested

40 ambitious : goals ::
  A worried : stress
  B eager : ideas
  C calm : energy
  D patient : fear

44 fork : eat ::
  A pen : pad
  B teacher : instruct
  C pencil : write
  D spoon : soup

41 arm : body ::
  A eraser : pencil
  B point : arrow
  C tail : tip
  D branch : trunk

45 bark : tree ::
  A grass : seed
  B core : apple
  C skin : body
  D coat : pants

42 food : full ::
  A drink : thirsty
  B weekday : holiday
  C knowledge : educated
  D choice : decision

46 cap : baseball ::
  A helmet : cycling
  B club : golf
  C head : jumping
  D puck : hockey

47 ocean : waves ::
  A desert : dunes
  B water : liquid
  C skin : body
  D water : fire

48 cookie : crumbles ::
  A paper : lines
  B pencil : sharpener
  C ice : melts
  D volcano : burst

49 crust : earth ::
  A question : test
  B bat : ball
  C heads : penny
  D peel : orange

50 criticize : mistake ::
  A study : textbook
  B congratulate : accomplishment
  C admire : painting
  D dice : onion

END

Test 2

Directions

Each question begins with two words. These two words go together in a certain way. Under them, there are four other pairs of words lettered A, B, C, and D.

Find the lettered pair of words that go together in the same way as the first pair of words.

1. band : musician ::
   A instrument : case
   B dog : pack
   C fish : school
   D herd : cow

2. melody : song ::
   A concert : harmony
   B musician : author
   C whistle : tune
   D plot : story

3. chariot : automobile ::
   A abacus : calculator
   B taxi : stagecoach
   C pencil : pen
   D plow : tractor

4. stem : flower ::
   A yarn : thread
   B petal : color
   C trunk : tree
   D paper : kite

5. short : height ::
   A fat : measurement
   B tall : width
   C weak : exercise
   D heavy : weight

6. work : earn ::
   A play : rest
   B sleep : live
   C eat : drink
   D study : learn

7 fog : hail ::
   A red : blue
   B cherry : fruit
   C paste : liquid
   D storm : thunder

8 sand : beach ::
   A grass : field
   B water : cup
   C beard : face
   D crumb : bread

9 fantasy : thriller ::
   A tragedy : sadness
   B poem : verse
   C article : newspaper
   D action : comedy

10 wild : wolf ::
    A damaged : junk
    B bear : dangerous
    C domestic : dog
    D silly : serious

11 symphony : notes ::
    A graph : bar
    B language : words
    C novel : short stories
    D sacred : ritual

12 eagle : soar ::
    A cat : meow
    B dolphin : swim
    C dog : bark
    D rat : run

13 lake : ocean ::
    A sea : river
    B water : ice
    C snack : meal
    D path : divide

14 noun : verb ::
    A summer : spring
    B building : window
    C bat : fruit
    D plug : hole

15 bee : hive ::

   A chairs : office
   B student : school
   C ant : barn
   D bird : nest

19 meal : chef ::

   A illness : doctor
   B store : clerk
   C building : bricks
   D painting : artist

16 cold : ice ::

   A hot : drink
   B soft : water
   C hard : problem
   D shiny : gold

20 trunk : car ::

   A beaver : plants
   B ingredients : recipe
   C ice cream : sundae
   D letter : ink

17 summer : sunburn ::

   A prison : freedom
   B classroom : confusion
   C party : excitement
   D winter : frostbite

21 police : protect ::

   A librarian : design
   B actor : sing
   C teacher : organize
   D doctor : treat

18 tall : short ::

   A large : small
   B soft : quiet
   C fat : long
   D little : brief

22 carrot : vegetable ::

   A lettuce : cabbage
   B farmer : plant
   C marker : tape
   D computer : electronic

23 bake : cake ::
   A roast : oven
   B toast : bread
   C stir : stick
   D fry : pan

27 church : prayer ::
   A party : win
   B home : house
   C store : food
   D school : learning

24 giggle : happy ::
   A frown : smile
   B sad : angry
   C cry : tears
   D moan : frustrated

28 forest : tree ::
   A desert : cactus
   B jungle : rain
   C prairie : soil
   D garden : bug

25 clench : fist ::
   A roll : back
   B turn : hips
   C hunch : shoulder
   D grit : teeth

29 plate : food ::
   A cup : drink
   B cheese : side
   C bean : stove
   D tray : ice

26 shiver : cold ::
   A dance : energetic
   B scream : frightened
   C sweat : hot
   D hurl : excited

30 mold : clay ::
   A roll : pastry
   B twist : turn
   C push : pull
   D scramble : egg

31 essay : nonfiction ::
    A sonnet : poetry
    B word : definition
    C novel : plot
    D actors : cast

32 exercise : gym ::
    A clap : auditorium
    B sit : car
    C sell : mall
    D eat : cafeteria

33 swift : fast ::
    A smooth : soft
    B tepid : hot
    C thin : long
    D sluggish : slow

34 tulip : flower ::
    A petal : leaf
    B banana : yellow
    C almond : nut
    D branch : tree

35 heart : beat ::
    A direction : compass
    B clock : tick
    C wheel : turn
    D ball : bounce

36 soak : sponge ::
    A slide : tube
    B rotate : compass
    C click : button
    D protect : lock

37 keyboard : typist ::
    A ball : player
    B stethoscope : doctor
    C vest : police
    D baton : runner

38 spread : scatter ::
    A multiply : add
    B push : pull
    C bully : support
    D separate : divide

39 destroy : demolish ::
  A win : lose
  B honest : secret
  C amend : change
  D attempt : succeed

40 fickle : mercurial ::
  A calm : hot
  B erratic : manageable
  C sprightly : tranquil
  D flaky : flighty

41 cookbook : recipes ::
  A film : reviews
  B manual : instructions
  C magazine : cover
  D museum : tours

42 stone : sculpture ::
  A mural : painting
  B opera : stage
  C canvas : easel
  D clay : pottery

43 vegetarian : meat ::
  A seller : profit
  B judge : order
  C mechanic : vehicles
  D pacifist : violence

44 crocodile : reptile ::
  A kangaroo : marsupial
  B dog : pet
  C kitten : puppy
  D cat : lion

45 gong : mallet ::
  A guitar : string
  B orchestra : batgon
  C drum : stick
  D clarinet : reed

46 riddle : puzzlement ::
  A comedy : stage
  B clown : costume
  C pun : meaning
  D jest : laughter

47 fire : heat ::
   A waiter : restaurant
   B sign : stop
   C skin : body
   D job : money

48 bank : money ::
   A drawer : wood
   B chest : dream
   C silo : grain
   D theater : line

49 slang : language ::
   A coin : change
   B silence : sound
   C chat : conversation
   D speech : dialogue

50 shard : pottery ::
   A splinter : wood
   B hair : wig
   C ash : fire
   D sand : beach

Answers

TEST 1

1	D	29	A
2	C	30	C
3	C	31	C
4	C	32	D
5	C	33	A
6	A	34	C
7	B	35	C
8	A	36	A
9	C	37	A
10	D	38	D
11	B	39	D
12	B	40	A
13	D	41	D
14	C	42	C
15	D	43	C
16	D	44	C
17	A	45	C
18	C	46	A
19	D	47	A
20	D	48	C
21	C	49	D
22	B	50	B
23	D		
24	C		
25	D		
26	C		
27	D		
28	B		

TEST 2

1	D	29	A
2	D	30	A
3	A	31	A
4	C	32	D
5	D	33	D
6	D	34	C
7	A	35	B
8	A	36	D
9	D	37	B
10	C	38	D
11	B	39	C
12	B	40	D
13	C	41	B
14	A	42	D
15	D	43	D
16	D	44	A
17	D	45	C
18	A	46	D
19	D	47	D
20	C	48	C
21	D	49	C
22	D	50	A
23	B		
24	D		
25	D		
26	C		
27	D		
28	A		

Good luck!

Made in the USA
Middletown, DE
15 April 2019